MW01104242

Bright Spots
&
Shadows

By China Corvino

Bright Spots & Shadows
Copyright © 2021 by China Corvino

All rights reserved. No part of this publication may be
reproduced, distributed, or transmitted in any form or
by any means, including photocopying, recording, or
other electronic or mechanical methods, without the prior
written permission of the author, except in the case of
brief quotations embodied in critical reviews and certain
other non-commercial uses permitted by copyright law.

Tellwell Talent
www.tellwell.ca

ISBN
978-0-2288-6076-1 (Paperback)
978-0-2288-6075-4 (eBook)

Introduction

I was in my early twenties when this collection of writing was born. As I look back through it now I see the early, the middle, and the late twenties all wound up together. Confused, confident, unsure, unsettled, hopeful, positive, sad, and a mind full of wonder while wandering aimlessly through a life I wasn't sure about at the time. Our twenties really give us the opportunity to be messy, to try things, to fail, to succeed, to fail and succeed and fail again. Mine were one of my greatest teachers. I was old enough to process the world around me with an open mind, but young enough to not have a clue what any of it meant, or would mean for my future. When putting together this book my mind drifted to two places. First, the lake my family's cottage sits by in Northern Ontario, Canada. Second, a large cenote I visited in Tulum, Mexico. Here's why. The lake up north is a dark, almost opaque blue. You can't see much through it though the water is spring fed and pure. Its bottom is a mix of mud, sticks, leaves, and sand, and so only at the very shallowest parts can you see through to what's below you. You have to jump in with the faith that nothing is there to hurt you. You can swim peacefully in it once you allow yourself to let go of that fear of the unknown, fear of the darkness, the shadows. The cenote is crystal clear. You can stand high above it or right next to it and see meters down into the clear, aqua blue waters to the rock formations below. You can see where the fish are, the deepest places, where you

want to go and where you might want to steer clear of.
It's enticing with its bright colours and clear visuals.
There is no worry of what might meet you down there as
you can see it for what it is, bright and clear and blue.
Sunlight sparkles off both bodies of water
magically, hypnotically. Both are beautiful
in completely different ways.
These are the two parallels you will find written between
these pages. The bright spots are the crystal clear aqua
blue waters that we can always look to when we're
feeling muddied, discouraged, in need of a vision of
calm, some clarity. The shadows are the rich dark blue
lake, with depth you cannot see and a body you must
trust will take care of you even if you can't always see
how. They are the teachers we must dive into in order
to grow, to learn, to become the people we are meant
to be, to be successful in our journey through life.

I hope you find yourself
in the bright spots & the shadows
One can't exist without the other
& we are meant to help each other

This book is dedicated to anyone & everyone who has ever found it difficult to express themselves unashamedly. Writing is my outlet, my way of process, of making & finding peace. I encourage you to find yours, hold it closely & use it. Reflect, refresh, & recharge through it.

Bright Spots

The world is full of bright spots
Bright people
bright scenery
bright work being done
You have to catch them & hold on to them
the moments that you notice
the moments when you feel it
because the storms will hit
the darkness will try to linger
& you will need some light to hold on to
when you can no longer see
You will need some memory to revive you
to remind you that it's not all bad
that the world isn't all so cruel
that there is beauty to be seen
life that lets you breathe
& the simple joy of finding something
in which you can believe
Remember the bright spots

I took a walk with you
through the daisy field
I was alone
but awareness bloomed
In every silken petal
I felt your skin
In every bit of yellow
I saw your spirit blink
Maybe you are dancing now
with the angels far away
but I know that you were with me
in the daisy field that day

Maybe I always say too much
or live my life too loudly
My heart is on my sleeve
it is embedded there soundly
Maybe I am reckless
or too much in the moment
My soul is a wanderer
& I have always known it
maybe my mind is twisted
or seems that way at times
rolled in light & darkness
I try not to look behind
Maybe I am challenging
or hard to understand
or difficult to hear
or impossible to mend
& even if all of these things are true
I get to choose who I'm becoming
& my darling
so do you

Take a break today
rest your mind up
stop the chase
Take a moment
just embrace
what you're feeling
don't escape
Close your eyes now
big deep breath
feel the air flow
through your chest
Let it all go
this is best
Take a break love
you need rest

Soft spring breezes are forever healing
a reminder that we're here
& breathing

In the midst of greater storms
a little old town eased my soul

I loved the way the moments felt
like time had no existence
The outside world could not reach us
no matter it's persistence
Nothing could get close to us to change how deep it was
& every second of our time was still never enough
There was this bond between us that
no one could understand
Together in our own world
hearts in each other's hands

In early evening
listening to birdsong
watching the sun sink slowly
the light on the tree line
the water sitting calmly
the wind has followed suit
everything about this moment
puts mind & soul at ease
Listening to nature
all its sounds & all its quiet
there is no better feeling
than the one of with the wild
One beat out in this place
just like all the others out there calling
Just a being in wilderness
blissful
watchful
alone
yet surrounded by a choir of living things
at this evening hour
This place is more magical than ever
my senses are fully tuned in
my body resting
soaking in all the glory around this little lake
This place that can never be replaced

Nobody took courage away from me
Kindness was a choice I'd make
over & over again
Even if I always lost
even if it broke my heart
I wanted to show love
I wanted to live honestly
with my words out on my sleeve
where people cared & met eyes
& our minds were free to speak

Thank you for always being the steady bedrock
in my crumbling limestone world
Even though you haven't always known it
you have been the one soul that I've never doubted
the one I know would save mine if it needed saving
Please remember that even when I am struggling
I am your kin
which means I will always figure it out
You taught me how to survive
You are the reason I survived things
I never thought that I could
You have always been my quiet life guard
protecting me when I didn't know I needed protection
& teaching me how to respect & honour myself
when my insecurities & anxiety have tried to take over
You always send me a message when I need it most
I don't know how you know
but you do
Thank you for existing
Thank you for being my friend
my family
& a horizon to follow in the darkest of storms
I am forever grateful for the bond we share
I love you endlessly & always

I think I've moved passed all the pain
Time is healing what I couldn't explain
With the fire I lost a piece
of who I was
for who I'd be
I found a whole new strength in me
A force before I couldn't see

My Dad once said to me
When it comes to dealing with human beings
expect to be disappointed
& you won't be
& every now & then
you'll be pleasantly surprised

I remember them
all of the moments
Yes the bad ones sting
& the good ones can too
Sometimes it all feels terrible
but then the past releases you
& the reliving of those moments
doesn't bite like it used to
It evolves into a lesson
each twinge of pain
becomes a guideline
of how you can keep living
So keep living

We want to understand each other's pain
but the truth is
we can't
We can empathize & imagine the hurt
but we can never feel someone else's sorrow
Only that person knows their wound
& feels it from the inside out
The best thing we can do
is understand
that we can't understand
& show love anyway
People need love anyway

I hope that we're all learning from each other
The more I hear their stories the more sense is made
This is why we are the way that we are
all of us
because of what we've experienced
We should cherish the bits of other's lives
& our own
the moments that changed them
changed us
because we change each other all the time
without even knowing it
We open the windows to our lives
& we save each other

promise me you won't forget the magic
when time comes to wear it away

Alone never really felt like lonely
& home never really felt that homey
Every time she saw the water she was free
as if the sky reflected in it
could simply fill her dreams
She was the type to find a different road
& places no one else would go
She wanted to leave her past behind
so she kept running
towards the northern line

she was everywhere
in those yellow trees
I made believe

Chase the moon until it fades
Soon the sun will rise again
Day & night
through dark & light
I've got you
Whether we end up safe or not
I'd travel the world to this very spot
I'd fight every battle over again
In all my stories
you're at the end

If it's all about the idea of someone
I promise that you will be disappointed
I promise that you don't know everything
in seeing pictures or posts or comments
in knowing someone from surface interactions
There is so much to the human mind
& if you assume anything
you will most likely be wrong
& don't ever be sorry
if you are not what they thought of you either
if you are not what they wanted you to be
You don't owe anyone that
You're living a life just like they are
trying to figure it out day by day
Remember that an image is never the whole picture
most of the story is never truly told
it's not often asked about either
I hope that you realize
comparison is condemning
judgement is juvenile
& both are a complete waste of time
Learn to expect less & appreciate more
Life is so much better when you let go
when you rise up & be yourself
your whole
true
self

I know you think that you don't deserve them
the small moments of happiness that you feel
while you are still recovering
but you do
You are given them in order to remember
that you are still here
that you are still breathing
that your heart is still beating
You are allowed to be loved
to feel love
to let the ice in your veins melt
for the life that you still have
the changes that you can embrace
the things that you can enjoy
I know you think it should be over
that it feels over because of what you've been through
but that isn't true
Once you see that
you will remember why you can choose to live fully
why you can let the happiness in
even if your mind tells you you're not good enough
even if your heart still weighs heavier than
the boulders that knocked you sideways
We all have the choice to change our futures
to open ourselves up again & let the light in
We all deserve the chances we are given
the love we are given
after the storms shipwreck us & break us & change us
We all deserve to see a calm sunrise again
the chance to make new paths
take new routes
& find our way to peace

There is no perfect remedy
or secret lullaby
There is only room to wander
under these changing skies
Remember when you told me
to meet you by the moon
I couldn't reach the sky yet
& you left all too soon
Well sometimes I still look for you
between the glowing clouds
before the universe swirls again
moving the light all around
I hope that you are still there
somewhere humming by the moon
& that you can hear the songs
I still sing for you

The miles don't matter
when the minutes fly by
one hand in yours
one out to the sky
On a sun soaked afternoon
or a morning drenched in rain
this love of ours stays warm
dancing on heart & brain

Street lamp bike rides & ice cream cones
making love & blue water coves
Memories engraved into our brains
the kind of love from which you're changed

We watched the moon that night
seated side by side
waiting for the stars to spark
to feel electric life
You played that beautiful music
you held my hand in yours
when the stars took up the sky
the universe was ours

There was nothing more beautiful in that moment
than the look on her face & the love in her eyes
It was warm enough to heat the sea
I could feel the jealousy from the sun
watching her bask in its light
gazes all steered her way
& she didn't notice
She just was
this incredibly light human being
with so much depth & sorrow
but you'd never know her pain
She lived to feel happiness
& she lived just to live
to be still at the waters edge
or splashing her feet running through the shallows
I'll never forget the first time I saw her
or the first time she spoke to me
I felt that to my bones
If she was a flower
I was a bee
instinctually drawn to her by nature
watching her every subtlety
admiring her grace & her beauty
the way she looked at life
& all of its monstrosities
With her it wasn't rose coloured glasses
it was a golden life
No matter the journey
alive & on fire
right in front of our eyes

The reason I get up off the floor when I am broken
The sunlight through my window on my darkest days
The fresh forest air after weeks in the city
The tingle of excitement that winds through my veins
The reason I smile & the cause of my laughter
The butterflies that drum in my stomach
The feeling of steadiness in my mind
The waves that carry me back to shore
The reason I breathe when I just might explode
The release into bliss after a really long day
The motivation to keep trying when
hope becomes distant
The courage to fight when the battle looks rough
The quiet smoke to my crackling fire
The light that chases off the shadows
The wild in my dreams & the calm in my nightmares
The look that holds me still for hours
The warm summer breeze after months in the cold
The morning to my midnight & the
midnight to my morning
It's love

I learned about steadiness that night
I was learning what he'd been through
& he spoke openly about it
I didn't ask a lot of questions
I didn't feel like I needed to
We were both away from home
& maybe the air had lightened my heart
or maybe it was the way he carried along with me
It was almost eerie
the way we fell into stride like that
There was no reason or feeling to be anything
other than exactly who we were
We didn't know what was about to happen
Our futures were entirely in limbo
especially then
It gave us the freedom to genuinely just be
to enjoy
I'd never known a person like him
someone I didn't need to question to get to know
We felt as we were & we were as we felt
moment to moment
I have been known to crave answers & seek out the depth
raw as it sometimes may be
but I didn't have to with him
Maybe we both wore our hearts on our sleeves
Maybe that's why it felt like home
I didn't worry about anything when I was near him
like something about him just clung to me
& I'd be lying if I said
I didn't cling a little back

I'll do whatever I can to make it known
even the saddest of hearts
are never alone

I am so thankful for those who never left
for all of those who have loved me
through my lowest & highest
madness & genius
failures & successes
& everything in between
Thank you for being here
for letting me know that my army is ready
whenever I can't do it alone
I am forever grateful for you

Ask for what you need
plant it
water it as seed
Let it sink in
let it breathe
You will receive
you will receive

This should be the end of the tears darling
This should be the moment when you look
to the sky & remember who you are
& why you deserve all that your dreams can dream up
This should be the time when you tell
yourself you are worth so much more
than the hurt you have received
Remember that you are not broken
you are changed
& you are here to learn
to love
to experience this body & this life
that is all
& even though it feels like your world has fallen apart
it is only the earth rotating
it is only what is here to teach you
even when you don't want to learn
even when you aren't ready
We have to suffer
to learn
We have to learn
to survive
& we have to break
to rebuild

There really is a magic hour
when nature comes alive
here within these warm months
all things unveil their prize
The light catches the leaves
the breeze blows through the petals
the birds all sing in chorus
a little piece of heaven

There are some people we just have to let go of
as difficult as it may be
It is possible to love someone & know
that distance is still the best thing
We cannot continue a healthy life
that welcomes healthy love
if we are always holding on to our past experiences
Let it go
Clear a space in your mind & your heart for something
someone
greater
meant for you
for your next moves in life
The past will always be a piece of us
but it is just a piece
it does not define what comes next
Learn not to expect
but to embrace
& allow the changes to happen
for better things are on their way
believe that

There was a looking glass
that only I could see
a small space that I found
for so long only me
Then one day you stepped through
& with you came a light
I thought this place was mine
then you came & made it bright
Hidden there I was
happy in solitude
but the roses didn't shine
like they did when they saw you
The sunshine became warmer
& the rains performed a dance
the grass was ever greener
nudging me to take a chance
I thought this was a hideout
to escape the world alone
& then you came reminding
that life is made to grow
There was a looking glass
so secret & so quiet
then you saw it too
& my heart could not deny it

You thought you were abandoned
by everyone before
My dear you couldn't stand it
to think you had no score
I'll tell you what they didn't
I'll show you that you're free
to achieve your own well being
to be more than what they see
You thought that you weren't worth it
you almost gave up the fight
because they said you're too much
you let them dim your light
Remember that you got here
past everything before
without a hand to hold
you became so much more
than anything they told you
than anything you thought
You grew to be a warrior
you overcame a lot
You thought you couldn't do it
did not think you'd see the end
of all the hurt they caused you
now you see that you can mend
Now you know that you are stronger
Now you know you've got the fight
Now you know they cannot harm you
Now you're shining so damn bright
You thought it wouldn't leave you
all the hurt that you have felt
Look at you now rising
past the hands that you were dealt

I will not let it catch me
The past I left behind
I'm up here with the birds now
Feeling wind beneath new life
I will let it teach me
Use it only to do better
Only to reach higher
To remember not to settle

Know that you are
& always have been
worthy of life
If you ever forget
I will be here to remind you
If you ever stumble
I will give you balance
If you ever get knocked down
I'll reach out to lift you up
& if you ever completely shatter
I will help you sweep up the pieces
& hold your hand
while you discover how you can
place it all back together
Because we all lose
& we all win
& when we do it together
we all become more whole
more human
more alive

somewhere
there is space
for a quiet sunrise
& thoughts as soft
as lullabies

I played on these strings
& thought of you
the things that you taught me
what they taught me too
I strummed through the verses
fingers sore but alive
I hoped you might hear it
so I tried not to cry
My voice grew much stronger
opened up like the sky
pouring out with emotions
the time passed on by
I kept with the music
my blood echoed yours
holding on to the moment
you stood in that door
The melodies drifted
chords dancing along
from that hollow instrument
out came your song

Respect & kindness should be valued more
Anger
jealousy
greed
manipulation
are all easy to collapse into
They are part of us as humans
the weakest sides really
Respect & kindness are learned
They are a challenge at times
They require more skill
more effort
more heart
Kindness is a challenge
rise to it

Light of the moon turn me
inside to see
that all of which I dream
I am capable to be

To be true to myself
I must rid myself of you
The weight that I feel near you
has grown solid & sticky
I can no longer pretend for your benefit
or comfort
The more I grow the less I feel that you do
& you wish that I could stay the same
but I cannot
I will not
I can love you
I will love you
but I must do it from over here now
where I am free & safe & happy
& you have room to grow on your own
this is a beautiful thing really
to separate for the sake of truth
true peace
true strength
true self
if you can't understand now
one day you will
& you'll feel the same air that I do
when I let go of what no longer deserves me
when I say no to what no longer serves me

little white butterfly
what spirit are you
I see you dancing
as iridescent wings do
Are you my grandmother
gliding by to kiss my cheek
Are you my mothers mother
the one that I did never meet
Are you a solo traveller
passing through to say hello
Are you a lost love my dear
as you land upon my toe
Whoever you are quiet soul
you're welcome in this garden
Bask among the flowers
no need to beg for pardon
Your presence brings me joy
You play such a great part
Thank you for coming to visit me
& lightening my heart

Find people that you can talk to
really talk to
Not the surface
pretend
put on a presentation about your life
& feelings type of talking
the real
raw
vulnerable
deep
honest
soul clearing type where you feel refreshed afterwards
Find people who leave you feeling inspired & encouraged
not weighted & unsure
In this life
this short
beautiful life that we are given
the biggest waste of time is spent playing a part
or putting on a show in order to fit in or be accepted
enough of that
When you find the right people those
things will just fall into place
& if you feel you cannot find it
hang out with yourself
make yourself happy
do your own thing
doing this will attract like minded people to you
once you find yourself
your people will find you
everyone else is just a lesson to help you get there

If I could take it all with me
there would be no room to see
so I leave space now for purpose
deeply grateful to have learned this

The obstacles we face
take their turn
take their place
& though it has been spoken
it is pain that breaks us open
it is heart that keeps on giving
it is love that keeps on winning
it is breath into our being
it is light & dark & grieving
The tests can be so tough
& still we don't give up
We learn to break the mould
Stop doing what we're told
Start doing what transcends us
& give time to things that mend us

There are no words enough
to explain all of the love
between family
between friends
inside love that never ends
amongst chaos
through the pain
threads entangled in our brains
stitches we can only feel
heartbeats aren't caged in steel
just fragile layers of moments
onto them we will keep holding
the little bits of glory
entangled in our stories

Wait for the one who honours you like a Queen
the one who you look at & see a King
Wait for the one who makes your heart dance
the one who you run to at every chance
Wait for the person who laughs by your side
the one who makes all of your dreams come alive
Wait for the one who comforts your tears
the one who erases all of your fears
Wait for the one who shows up every time
the one who believes in you & always tries
Wait for the one who ignites your fire
the one who makes you twist with desire
Wait for the soul who compliments yours
the one who never closes their door
Wait for the magic that you know is love
the kind of authenticity you couldn't make up
Wait for the one who romances you
the one who does sweet things out of the blue
Wait for the one who talks & who listens
the one with whom you've never resisted
Wait for the one who kisses you softly
the one who gives you butterflies often
Wait for the one who loves faithfully
the one that makes you see differently
Wait for the one who understands your flaws
the one who surprises you just because
Wait for the one you can't live without
the one that you would never doubt
Wait for the one that knows your worth
the one who always puts love first
Wait for the one that sees you for you
the one that for anything you would do
Wait for the one who's so humble & kind
the one you can never get off of your mind
Wait for the one you'll tell stories with

the one who helps you through all of life's shifts
Wait for the one that is meant to be
the one person you know would never leave
Wait for the one that helps you feel steady
that space in your heart has always been ready

Shadows

I can feel all of my seams
torn slightly
ready to rip
I can't sew this back together
like the button on his shirt
Nothing is forever
everything is temporary
I know that
I keep learning that

You want the easy answer
the easy option
& those are plentiful
to your left & right
take your pick of them
I am not the easy choice
I am not the easy path
I am not easy to find
because there is no copy
& I can't be yours
You didn't really want me
you wanted something
something easier maybe
& you will find it
but you won't forget
the bits you ignored
the fear that won
that tore me away
You will remember
the girl who cared for you
against all odds
You will feel I am gone
& you will wonder
what may have been
if you'd only let it be
if you'd only taken a chance
with your heart
instead of your head

there will always be surprises
life is like that
some of them will shake your character
& test your beliefs
others will tear you to pieces
that can never be put back the same way again

I looked for you
when the curtains closed
but you weren't there
& so it goes
in a room full of people
I still felt alone

she was the magic
but you wanted to be the wand

There were days the laughter just came easy
though that was years ago
Time took so much away from us
but it kept giving more of itself too
We were facing an inescapable battle
to find ourselves
in a sea full of waiting daggers & masked personas
The only thing we knew was movement
& we never
ever
stopped

Life is a waterfall
both beautiful
& punishing

In a moment
everything I knew had evaporated
What was left were two humans
two individuals
with no idea how to come back from
the losses they'd been dealt
I watched as everything separated
This was starting over

I have fought battles worse than this
& have always come out alive
I have forgiven worse than you
& still I have survived

I rolled the dice
& saw your eyes
Where I was naked
you wore disguise

She didn't smile
he didn't laugh
He didn't notice
she didn't dance
She didn't cry
he didn't care
He didn't want it
it wasn't fair
She didn't stumble
he didn't fall
They didn't know
I saw it all

Making promises he couldn't keep
but I believed the fantasy
red flags flying
I pretended not to see

When it's dark
& I can't sleep
I'm stuck inside
a memory
Close my eyes
count the sheep
Still awake
& only me

There are times in my life that I look back
on & have no idea who that person was
the one making those choices
the one lost in a fog
I feel like my pain took over & was operating my
entire being while my mind just rolled on
I could never catch up to myself in time
I didn't realize how hurt I was until I
crawled my way out of the haze
My mind was so full of thoughts that
I wouldn't let myself think
& so my system overloaded
It crashed
It was only once that happened that I could hit
the reset button & remember who I really was
or am
Me
I am me
Not what has happened to or around me

All the things I cannot change
no matter the time
or number of days
Wants & needs are blurred a bit
& I can't speak a word of it

We just kept driving
it left my mind clear
knew skeletons were following
but didn't feel fear

I'm sorry I never told you
when things weren't okay
I'm sorry I couldn't tell you
everything inside my brain
I'm sorry I got scared
& that I didn't stay
I'm sorry I couldn't listen
& that I caused you pain
I'm sorry I couldn't tell you
what I needed to say
I'm sorry I made you angry
& couldn't take it away
I'm sorry for the confusion
& for acting a little strange
I'm sorry I didn't open up
I just felt so restrained
I'm sorry that I lied
when I said this was all a game
I'm sorry that I left you
when I could have found a way
I'm sorry if I used your heart
I take all of the blame
I'm sorry I didn't call you back
to say I wasn't the same
I'm sorry I couldn't let you in
everything had changed
I'm sorry I never told you
or if I made you feel ashamed
I'm sorry I didn't show my love
when yours was all ablaze

We hung up the phone
you were crying
& I was crying
& everything was gone
just like that
I knew we'd never get back
to the time before that call
the one that changed us forever
it was august
almost fall
The loss was just too much
the breakdown was too hard
We were never strong enough
to recover from it all

All of me
spread thin around
Energy shifting
sinking ground
Hello old ways
I thought you'd gone
I guess you've been here
all along

Love
or lust
or loneliness
attention seeking ghosts of this
what drove you in
what drove you out
what keeps you darling
what keeps you
Pain
or hurt
or giving in
living out loud
living within
causing rage
seeping sin
what keeps you
Look on past out to the sea
all the motion life can be
I know that you will never see
what keeps you
Cut the ties & still they live
no one dies
but all must give
pieces of their heart & all that keeps them

I love you
but I'll run from you
so that you will never see
this little patched up heart
the deepest depths of me

We overthink the things that we are insecure about
& sometimes we let those insecurities take over
to the point where we aren't sure what's real
we're just so afraid that the ones we love
won't love us the way that we really are
so we hide behind masks that we make
in terribly crafted false realities
where we never feel like enough
so we forget how to be loved

I wonder if they'll ever see me
or if I'll ever really let them
I know it's me that built these walls
It's not their fault
I forgot to install any windows

You're not the only one
who jumped too soon
fell too fast
& never carried landing gear

I loved you most at night
When I could barely see myself

I'm not the kind of person you can fix
I know you didn't ask for this

Forgetting to live now
lost along the journey
I wonder why
towards these mundane things
we are supposed to hurry

I was myself
but broken in pieces
I was everywhere
but couldn't reach what I needed
I wanted people
then wanted no one at all
I'd be trying to rise
then I'd let myself fall
I became reckless
maybe out of control
I didn't think anyone
could understand my soul

You are not stupid
for following your heart
into a trap your eyes couldn't see
It doesn't make you foolish
to have trusted in another
You are not wrong for breaking
when they broke your heart

Maybe this is just a feeling I have
to feel over & over again
Maybe I'm not ready to learn whatever this lesson is
because learning it would mean I have to really let you go
It means I have to ignore all of the
instincts that pull me towards you
It means I have to pretend I don't feel
the things that I feel for you
It means I have to practice how to live
in a world where you do not exist
One day I will make it to that place
where I understand why this was all just a part of the ride
the test
the journey
One day I'll understand why you had to go

When she was gone I still felt her near
I could smell her perfume
but couldn't release another tear
I knew nothing would ever be the same
so out loud softly
I said her name
I wanted her to send the rain
Who I was before
no longer remained

I'm not sure how we got here
Silence is our new best friend
This isn't how it started
but it is how it will end
I don't know how it changes
where everything feels distant
like we were lost in a moment
one we weren't meant to be given
I no longer feel confused
I know too much these days
when I see something is gone
it's just time to walk away

For all the times I looked at you & saw a golden heart
For all the times you looked away & tore my head apart
For all the bullshit games you played
& words you flung around
For all the empty promises left scattered on the ground
For every kindness I gave & the lies you threw in return
For everything I swallowed
I know better now
I've learned

All of this baggage
carried down through time
all of us suffering
all of us saying we're fine
History cracks through these walls
we can't stop it from showing
So the pretenders run
& the realists brace
whatever comes next
we all have to face

I was staring up at the pine trees
black silhouettes against the cloudy evening sky
I thought I saw you there sitting in the branches
but you couldn't see me
you didn't notice I was watching
I saw you gazing out over the lake
observing the wind on the water
I swore I saw your chest rising & falling
as if you were really there
breathing
listening
but you weren't
you weren't

I had reached a certain point
where I just did not want to start
I'd been burned so many times
I began to fear the spark

Could you go
leave me be
There's nothing here
nothing to see
Close the door
I'll hit the light
Sink into darkness
black as night
Please don't watch
don't ask me why
Please don't listen
don't hear me cry
You don't know me
why I am this way
You never will
you'll never stay
It's all too much
while not enough
Never steady
always rough
I'm alone
& it's okay
Need to be still
somewhere away
Lost is my mind
adrift flows my heart
Wanting an end
wanting a start
Please walk on
let me fade out
Away from the lies
all of the doubt
I am broken
you won't understand
I'm in my own arms

holding my own hand
On the other side
the door is locked
Emotions quiet
I can't talk
This is the truth
right here & it's raw
I'm human at best
not what you saw

A majority of sadness
that is never spoken of
All bleeding in silence
with a false sense
that it's saving the others

I used to cause trouble for myself
because I thought it was fun
to live recklessly
out loud
burning rubber
tire marks on the pavement
I no longer knew how to enjoy
I had used the joy up trying to escape in it
I no longer had fun
I had moments
& then I'd run

Monday afternoon
tired from staying up
howling at the moon
You were here just yesterday
then yesterday took you away
& I'm holding on
to a way back
where we felt whole
we were on track
Now the whispers in the street
say that it's true
that my heart was always gambled
with you

The dress & all of it was just a ruse
so that you would see in me
the version that I'd choose

We want to think that people will treat us
with the same love that we give to them
but that's not always the way it happens
We have to learn to walk away when the
hurt rushes in like dark clouds
We have to know we did our best
& that we cannot control the storm

For a long time
I didn't want nice
I wanted rocks thrown
& broken windows
that cracked open my pain
so it had somewhere to escape from

This thing that we do
there's me
there's you
so connected
so distant too

They're afraid
just like me
afraid of what everyone
wants us to be

Just one more time
we both say
then promise to keep
our hearts locked away

I woke up one day & saw what I was doing to myself
over & over again
I was standing in the centre of a wildfire
& expecting not to get burned
I was giving the same chances out
& expecting not to get hurt
So I told myself no more
No more chances
No more expectations
No more
I wasn't going to give them anymore of myself
Then I went on a mission to get back
all the parts of me that I lost
trying to rescue people who didn't
care if I drowned saving them

That's just the way they are
That's just the way we are
We were born with it in blood
Forever in search
of what we think is love

It's possible that I hung on to all of the bad ones while
dismissing all of the good ones as just not right
It's possible that I let great loves walk away while
clinging to the ones who were breaking me
I will never get to know about the ones I threw away &
I will never forget about the ones I stuck around for
when I knew I never should have given those chances
It's possible that I've made all the wrong choices so far
but it's also possible that I've finally learned from it
I can't do anything about the past
but I can do something about the now
I can pay more attention
I can stop letting the hurt rule over the healing
I can give the good ones a chance to really know me
I was always just afraid that they would be too good
too unbroken
to understand the broken in me
but I never gave them a real shot
Maybe the good ones have darkness too
like me
Maybe there are ones like me

How could you not see
that everything you did
left scars all over me

Every time you came back
I let you
& I knew what would happen
because the record broke long ago
I told myself so many lies to defend you
to make you out to be someone that you weren't
someone trustworthy
someone true
& every time you played a game
I played too didn't I
I had a piece
I moved it around
but you were cheating
you tricked me
You told me it was a different game
so I would make all the wrong moves
because you never wanted us to win
You just wanted to see how long I'd play

There you are
in my head
for no reason
with no meaning
you still appear
though far from near
I fear
that you won't leave
Like part of me
you'll always be
returning
a bad dream

I still wear the mask I made
even though I use it less
I am still aware
I know
that I'm not doing my best
It's not easy to say
even less easy to be
living somewhere
in between

It feels like a stab in the chest
when the news breaks of a loss
the air escapes your lungs
your blood
your brain
everything is disorienting
like you're falling down
with nothing to grasp onto
For a second you think it couldn't be
that the hurt
the dizziness
the confusion
will stop
but it doesn't
You feel everything & nothing
You scream & no sound follows
Even after years have passed
you still remember that moment
These are the ones
I'd like to forget

You existed in my life like clouds
When you were thick & heavy you would stay
& once you felt light & airy
you'd float off & away

I won't forget the lesson I learned
when we broke
& I was the only one who shattered

You didn't have to do that
reach out then disappear
I hadn't forgotten your existence
& that's all you wanted to hear

Maybe you knew
what was going on
when you walked in
I was playing a song
You asked me if I couldn't sleep
I lied & told you I had a bad dream
I wanted you to leave just then
so I could be alone again
to figure out all of my thoughts
I couldn't tell you
about it all

Call me the fool
for I am always feeling fire
where there is ice
for I am always finding solace
in a love that cuts like knives
Call me a broken mind
to feel at once so strong
& yet slice up so easily
when that sweet blade comes along

It begins with you & me
& words spoken
soft
poetically
then experience changes
& chance takes its shape
& memories break
& emotions shake
every part shifts
& the world seems to quake
when what was before
makes a silent escape

we don't have a path
but we do have a story

You didn't make sense to me
You never did
you still don't
I could've not said anything
I could've let you reach out without a word back
I responded with a smile
because I'm different than you are
I responded with friendliness
because I don't wish you any pain
Some might call that weak
but I see it as strength
Some might call it giving in
but I see it as letting go
When I chose to speak the truth
you chose to try & hurt me
When I asked you for answers
you left me in question
I feel satisfaction not in revenge
but in forgiveness
I feel resolve not in anger
but in understanding
Not one of us really knows what we're doing
Not one of us knows what tomorrow
will bring or take away
I will choose the path that welcomes love
I will choose the words that express kindness over hate
You may not understand the way I react
& the way I let go
You may see everything differently than I do
& that's okay
You hurt me
but you also made me more aware
You took advantage of my heart
but you also forced me to open it again
Where you reacted with denial

I reacted with honesty
When you chose hate
I chose peace
When the desire to get even comes knocking
I simply don't answer it
When pride & ego try to take over
I ground myself again & again

I can forgive without forgetting
It's how I've learned to move on
I can show kindness & love
Even when I've been done wrong
It's that strength inside me
that gives me limitless power
to know that I've got myself
even in my darkest hours
I'll always take the high road
even if others won't meet me there
I'm going to keep my chin up
even when things don't seem fair
I'll smile when I feel like crying
& I'll never stop the fight
Even when I'm challenged
I'll find a way to make it right
I'm counting on my gracefulness
in putting my pride aside
to get me through the tests
that life will always provide

You took a part of me that night
I'll never be able to forget
I don't know why you did it
but I'll never get it back now
I gave into you & all that you are
I let myself pretend it was okay
but you're not free
I let myself fall with you
no cautions & no concerns
I didn't want it to end
& you couldn't let it pass you by
All we've ever had are these moments
ones that have consumed my mind
Every reason I have to run
& yet I stay
I'm keeping my distance now
maybe that will make it easier
I wonder if I took a part of you too
There's a chance you saw it in my eyes
how our connection burned like fire
For that time nothing else mattered
Maybe it stuck with you too
Maybe we can meet one day
& give each other back those pieces
the ones we took
when neither of us had anything to give away

It felt like we were meant to live that way
fast & free & in the moment
That's how we were together
So I try to let go of the bad shit
& remember those moments between us
because that's all that matters in the end
The good memories that never seem to leave
are brought to life with every photo
from a time when it felt effortless
from a moment when I felt happy
& I think you did too

I've heard a lot of stories about myself
but so very few that are true
Why is it that fiction spreads like wild fire
& the truth stays stagnant
hidden away
I learned to try & ignore the whispers
I tell myself it doesn't matter
because I know the truth
Then one of these stories appears
& my insides just crack like thin ice
all the feelings of vulnerability turn up
& there I am
right back like the first time it hit me
Why does no one doubt the source
What makes me a target for them
It makes me want to shut myself off
mute myself out so they can't hear
If I have no story there's no story to change
but that wouldn't stop them from fabricating anyway
So how do I get away from it
the picture they've painted of me is theirs
it also belongs to all those who believe it
That part hurts
My past is always inescapable
I have a hard enough time with the real stuff
the fake stuff just adds weight to the pack
It matters because I wear my heart on the outside
& I'm broken every time because of it
I'm so open & honest I forget to protect myself
It's like someone just beat me senseless
when I hear the bullshit
from the mouth of a friend
You know the ones
where it rips your gut out
because you never thought they'd believe the lies

until they're right next to you
repeating word for word the chosen tale
as if it's catching you off guard
When all you feel is defeated
Once again
the story wins
The truth tucked away
in plain sight

Tried my best not to cry
made effort to keep my chin lifted
told my feet one step at a time
when the past showed up tonight
It carried rumours
reminders of dark places
places I never want to go again
It won again tonight
I broke a little at the sound
of another story told in vein
so someone else could look cool
so someone else could play the victim
The expense is always character
Cheapening a reputation
for a purpose unknown
It hurts when it first hits my ears
incapacitating when it resurfaces
Trust becomes so hard
These are the moments that close me
turn me inside to hide
From smiling to shattered in seconds
There's nothing I can do
I can't take words from people's mouths
can't erase perceptions neatly fabricated
So I shut myself down
I have to close off to survive it
The wash of tears threatens my eyes
I won't let them out
even when I want to

My physical goes into a numb state
where everything hurts
but I can't feel
everything pulses
but nothing moves
I guess I'll never escape this place
where trust is scarce & lies are plentiful
where the past is always back to visit
my person always a target
It is a formula for madness

I can't pretend to be the person that you want
The person that you see is not who I am as a whole
You've forgotten that I'm just like you
I'm strangled by life violently
& often
The mask I wear is one I've worked on for years
Even when I've let you in
you didn't want any deeper than that mask
You wanted the amount of me that you could handle
the rest was & is mine to live with
Because no one wants to see the darker parts
they want the happy side
the charm
& I can't always give it to them
The shattered bits are too prominent at times
I can't hide them
& you'll see
That's when you'll laugh like it's a joke
to make yourself more comfortable than anything
& I'm left there sunken in it
alone
I don't want your attention
I want to feel completely human with someone
madness
faults
mistakes
The pressure to always show the good side is exhausting
I'm so tired of putting on for your benefit
I guess this is the point where I change
because so many I trusted broke the bond at the seams
as soon as my weaknesses came out of hiding

One day you're going to realize that people
cannot & will not ever stop hurting you
There are ones who will do it with so much
intention that you think you're going to break
Don't
They will try to tell you who you are
they will try to make you believe that
their way is the only way
& their thoughts are the only ones of value
Run
They will come in the form of friends
of family members
lovers
colleagues
& even strangers
Be aware & beware
Stay ready for the fall
& you can land it
But not without scars
The cuts will leave their mark on you forever
no matter how they fade
They want your attention
& they want the advantage
They'll wait for the glint in your eye that is trust
or hope
or love
& they will make their move to crush it
It's the only way they can feel good
It could be that that's all they ever wanted
to take from you without you ever
realizing what they'd really stolen

To breathe in every essence of your being
then spit it out into the world as nothing
as if you're no one
Maybe that's what they needed
The satisfaction of the crime committed
the knowledge that they broke you
in the wake of their actions
These people exist
but you can see through them eventually
Watch for it

Watching you
watching me
What is it
that this will be
Are you here
is this real
tell me how
you really feel
Don't get scared
don't close your heart
we can make it
or fall apart
I can feel you
figuring too
trying to sort out
what to do
There's something here
but we don't know
will it die
or will it grow
Each day is different
the emotions change
something about you
tells me to stay
But for how long
can I keep up
with this game
when does it stop
Can I relax
when you are here
I am trying
to drown the fear
Sometimes it wins
sometimes it loses

Most of the time
it's me who chooses
I really thought
that this could be
my happy ending
I did believe
Then something changed
& so did you
I wanted to run
but I couldn't move

We had one last conversation
it wasn't a goodbye
it was a bit of a fight
one I don't think we'll ever win
Time apart now
Silence between us now
That's what we need
Maybe we have a someday
but I know it's not tomorrow

Tell me about a time
when everything was fine
when your heart wasn't broken
& you felt full in your life
Please share with me your story
& open up my eyes
to the things that I am missing
to what I cannot realize
Show me how you do it
how you always can survive
when the world seems like it's dying
& it's hard to feel alive

Did you ever find your way back
From that place that you sunk yourself into
Where you told yourself nobody cared
because you didn't care
Did you finally find your truth
the one you always sought after
Or did you find contentment in hiding
the same way that I used to
the same thing I tried to save you from
That's the tricky thing about love
You can't save yours from the pain
They have to learn their truths themselves
& your love means nothing
until they love themselves

False romances & short story loves
late night entrances & sins in the sun
It all gets old eventually
there's no high left in the temporary

I found a way to shut myself off from all
of the things they have told me
to let myself know that their words are not the truth
that they just want to paint a picture for me to love
& then smear all the paint before it's dry
Now it's just a messy canvas
a representation of the chaos they created & relished in
I'm getting better at catching them though
getting better at seeing it coming
So it hurts a little less now

Darkest of nights
filled with pollution
Fast beating hearts
& quiet confusion
Using each other
to create this illusion
Leading the lost
to temporary solution
Finding a safe place
beyond inclusion
The troubling world
of human collusion

CPSIA information can be obtained
at www.ICGtesting.com
Printed in the USA
BVHW041932050122
625549BV00013B/875

9 780228 860761